It's a Girl Thing

Random Thoughts On Surviving Womanhood

BY MELISSA SOVEY

WILLOW CREEK PRESS

Published by Willow Creek Press, Inc.
P.O. Box 147, Minocqua, Wisconsin 54548

Photo Credits:

© ClassicStock/Masterfile:
p6, p12, p15, p24, p40, p47, p48, p51, p52, p63, p68, p72, p76, p79, p83, p84, p87, p91, p96

© imagebroker/Masterfile:
p8, p11, p16, p19, p20, p27, p28, p31, p32, p35, p36, p43, p56, p71, p81, p88, p92, p95

© SuperStock/Masterfile:
p39, p44, p55, p59, p64, p75

Design: Donnie Rubo
Printed in Canada

"To be a woman is something so strange, so confusing, and so complicated that only a woman could put up with it."

—Soren Kierkegaard

For all the special women in our lives who inspire and care for us, who bring us love, laughter and wonderful memories. For Beth, Lori and Maggie, the glorious Tweesters.

No two women are exactly alike.

"Sentences that begin with
'all women' are never, never true."

—Margaret Culkin Banning

However, there are some things all women have in common, and a few universal truths important to surviving womanhood.

"Always remember that you are absolutely unique. Just like everyone else."

—Margaret Mead

You're as young as you feel. Pick an age and stick to it. It's your womanly prerogative.

"She was a handsome woman of forty-five and would remain so for many years."

—Anita Brookner

Nobody else belongs in the driver's seat of your life. So put the pedal to the metal and take charge of that beast.

"If you want a high performance woman,

I can go from zero to bitch

in less than 2.1 seconds."

—Krystal Ann Kraus

Stop asking "who's the fairest one of all?" If you don't consider yourself The Queen, who will? That leading-lady-inner-voice is calling loud enough to wake the neighbors. Write your own fairy tale.

"A sobering thought: what if, at this very moment, I *am* living up to my full potential?"

—Jane Wagner

Be creative. Find alternatives
when life throws you road blocks.

"I would love to speak a foreign language, but I can't.

So I grew hair under my arms instead."

—Sue Kolensky

There's no time like the present. Don't ask if the glass is half full or half empty. Ask "Are you going to drink that?" Carpe Diem, Diva!

"Seize the moment.

Remember all those women on the *Titanic*

who waved off the dessert cart."

—Erma Bombeck

Take chances, be daring, and act as if it were impossible to fail. Shoot for the moon and take your sisters along for the ride.

"There is a microscopically thin line between being brilliantly creative and acting like the most gigantic idiot on Earth. So what the hell, leap."
—Cynthia Heimel

Live the life that pleases you. Some women are nature girls, some women rank camping on a fun scale right up there with an annual pap smear.

"To put it rather bluntly, I am not the type who wants to go back to the land; I am the type who wants to go back to the hotel."

—Fran Lebowitz

Repeat often: Yes, I am all that.

"The question isn't

who is going to let me;

it's who is going to stop me."

—Ayn Rand

Wear whatever you like. Attitude is your finest accessory.

(Apparel warning: Wearing skin-tight leather will leave you meaner than a girl on her fourth day of a diet. That moo is actually a cry for help.)

"Oh, never mind the fashion.
When one has a style of one's own,
it is always twenty times better."
—Margaret Oliphant

Self-reliance can never be underestimated. Offer subtle reminders to the doubtful that you are perfectly capable of taking care of yourself.

"There is no such thing as being too independent."

—Victoria Billings

Get uppity. Sometimes you've got to kick some serious ass. I'm just sayin'.

"Never grow a wishbone, daughter, where your backbone ought to be."

—Clementine Paddleford

Bouts of hedonistic revelry are key to surviving womanhood. Your peeps will understand. Everyone else will just have to be jealous.

"I'm a girl from a good family who was very well brought up. One day I turned my back on it all and became a bohemian."

—Brigitte Bardot

Appreciate your family, imperfections and all. Quirky is much better than perfect anyway. Just tell everyone your family puts the "fun" in dysfunctional.

"I think a dysfunctional family
is any family with more
than one person in it."
—Mary Karr

We're not all in touch with our inner Julia Child. Try mastering the art of one-dish-baked meals. If anyone complains, ask them if they'd like to know why you call your specialty dishes "kickassaroles."

"Life is too short to stuff a mushroom."

—Shirley Conran

Okay, you can easily survive womanhood without ever knowing the answer to this question, yet it is one that eludes nearly all of us. How in the hell are you supposed to fold a fitted sheet?

"Behind every working woman is an enormous pile of unwashed laundry."

—Barbara Dale

Say good-bye to the kids for awhile. Appreciate your girl's night out. But do be grateful for the youngsters in your life. Without them you'd never know how well Chardonnay goes with mac and cheese.

"Wine could become a place rather than a beverage."

—Morgan Llywelyn

Darlings, life has its scary moments. Like, your bejeepers have left the building scary. But, keep things in perspective. Remember, real horror is bathing suit shopping.

"Your mind is a dangerous neighborhood and you shouldn't go in there alone at night."

—Christiane Northrup

Listen to your inner grandmother. She'll tell you that sulking only serves two purposes, 1) deepening those furrows between your eyebrows and 2) nothing. (It's okay to ignore some of her advice like "cupcakes are not breakfast food.")

"Flops are part of life's menu and I've never been a girl to miss out on any of the courses."

—Rosalind Russell

There are days that bring a woman to her knees and make her cry big fat girly tears. Let the cork out of the bottle and let 'em flow. A good crying jag leads to new perspectives. Like a rainbow after a downpour.

"No more tears now;

I will think about revenge."

—Mary Queen of Scots

Girlfriend Therapy: Where *whining* is not permissible, but *wining* is encouraged, and you will always be reminded that bad decisions make good stories. A little chick-chat is way better than years of psychoanalysis.

"Going into therapy doesn't guarantee poop on toast."

—Laura Schlessinger

When things get really crazy, try posting Daily Affirmations where you'll see them first thing in the morning. Try this womantra:
I am at one with my multiple mood swings.

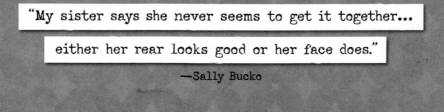

"My sister says she never seems to get it together... either her rear looks good or her face does."

—Sally Bucko

Sometimes there's just no substitute for a little self-image reinforcement from the cosmetic aisle.

"Beauty, to me, is about being comfortable in your own skin; that, or a kick-ass red lipstick."

—Gwyneth Paltrow

Of course no matter the question,
shoes are the answer.

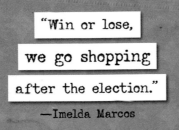

"Win or lose,

we go shopping

after the election."

—Imelda Marcos

There's no glory in being a nutritional overachiever. Occasional splurging is good for the soul. Never ignore a chocolate craving.

"Chocolate isn't like premarital sex.

It will not make you pregnant.

And it always feels good."

—Lora Brody

There are multiple reasons to get plenty of exercise. Top of the list; some things just aren't that pretty. Take elastic waistbands for instance.

"I'm not into working out.

My philosophy: no pain, no pain."

—Carol Leifer

Of course, there are other ways of augmenting your natural attributes. Your womanly bits belong to you, so be happy with them. Mother Nature doesn't always get things right. Otherwise, why would men have nipples?

"Some people think having large breasts makes a woman stupid.

Actually, it's quite the opposite:

a woman having large breasts makes men stupid."

—Rita Rudner

Stop blaming those spite-filled last five pounds for your lack of thinner peace; it's the unattainable air-brushed magazine images we should be dissing.

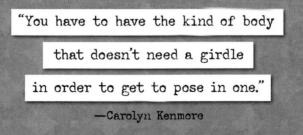

"You have to have the kind of body that doesn't need a girdle in order to get to pose in one."

—Carolyn Kenmore

Double standards be damned.
Why let the men, biker chicks
and cowgirls have all the fun?

"Nymphomaniac: a woman as obsessed
with sex as an average man."

—Mignon McLaughlin

After all, each new day provides
an opportunity to start fresh.

"When the sun comes up,
I have morals again."

—Elayne Boosler

In case your mother never told you, good taste is not just on the tip of your tongue. Timing is everything in the seduction department.

"There are times not to flirt: when you're sick, when you're with children, and when you're on the witness stand."

—Joyce Jillson

Don't think of your womanly guile as MANipulation. Foxiness has a much better ring to it.

"Give a man a fish and he has food for a day; teach him how to fish and you can get rid of him for the entire weekend."

—Zenna Schaffer

The moment you decide his nickname should be His Royal Heinie, it's time to pack up the picnic and find yourself a fresh new guy with the tags still on.

"Going out with a jerky guy is kind of like having a piece of food caught in your teeth. All your friends notice it before you do."

—Livia Squires

Every woman should have one gal in her friend arsenal that tells her not to hit the snooze button on her wake-up call too many times. She's the one who reminds you of your grandma and is likely to say to your soon-to-be ex, "Here's your hat, what's your hurry?"

"Breaking up is a time for moving on, not for writing your history in indelible ink."

—Johanna Newell

Remember: bad boys get you nowhere and you deserve better than a guy routinely outsmarted by cheese. So, should you have some kamikaze inclinations toward second chances, resist them.

"When you get back together with an old boyfriend, it's pathetic. It's like having a garage sale and buying your own stuff back.

—Laura Kightlinger

Appreciate every little moment that makes you feel special. And brag about it.

"No matter how happily a woman may be married, it always pleases her to discover that there is a really nice man who wishes she were not."

—Mary Catherine Bateson

Taking a break from the household chores restores the soul. Repeat after me: I'm not messy, I'm a genius.

"Procrastination isn't the problem, it's the solution. So procrastinate now, don't put it off."

—Ellen DeGeneres

We all have those days where we warn others not to phone, e-mail or make eye-contact with us under any circumstances. These are great times for personal reflection.

"Isn't it interesting how the sounds are the same for an awful nightmare and great sex?"

—Rue McClanahan

Keep your sister—centricity tight. Nuff said.

"Your sister is the only creature on earth

who shares your heritage, history,

environment, DNA, bone structure,

and contempt for stupid Aunt Gertie."

—Linda Sunshine

Women know how to weather the storms in life. When things get rocky and life screams, "brace yourself for impact" you can count on a woman to help you through it.

"Just when you think you've graduated from the school of experience, someone thinks up a new course."

—Mary H. Waldrip

Take spontaneous trips with gal pals. Go somewhere where the music is all about dancing, someone else does all the cooking, and the beverage of choice is champagne.

"Life loves to be taken by the lapel and told: 'I am with you, kid. Let's go.'"

—Maya Angelou

The Force of the Sisterhood of Womanhood
is a powerful one indeed. Latch on to it.

"The most beautiful discovery true friends make

is that they can grow separately

without growing apart."

—Elisabeth Foley

Find something to laugh about, something to be thankful for, and some nugget of wisdom to enrich your life every single day. Your girlfriends are great sources for all three.

"A good friend is a connection to life—

a tie to the past, a road to the future,

the key to sanity in a totally insane world."

—Lois Wyse

Celebrate you.